HUBBELL'S HOG HEAVEN

&

LIZ'S HAPPY HENS

A Farm Tour:

Korean Natural Farming Methods in Pahoa, Hawaii

by

Elizabeth Cannon

2013

A special thank you to my daughters who contributed in their unique ways with this bookwriting project. I could not have done it without their help, and I likely would have given up the entire thing long ago.

Lori Hubbell Meeker, thank you so much for all the help with editing, your great suggestions for improving my work, and your enthusiastic encouragement. If there are still any mistakes here, it's certainly not due to any lack on your part.

Kerry Montana Hubbell, thank you for sharing your wonderful photography. You have a good eye for detail and a generous soul. Many of the photos in this book are yours, and I am so grateful.

Table of Contents

Acknowledgements

Cho Global Natural Farming (CGNF), a method utilizing Indigenous Micro-Organisms (IMOs), was developed in South Korea by Master Han-Kyu Cho. Master Cho had been ridiculed for 40 years in his own country until fairly recently when younger, more progressive leaders (like the two mayors we met on our Korea trip, and even the President of South Korea) began to take his message of Natural Farming to heart. Since then, CGNF model farms and farmer's co-ops have been developed throughout the southern districts of South Korea, where the main growing areas are situated.

Dr Hoon Park brought attention to this method to Hawaii, and he continues to spread the word here, as well as to other parts of the world, through lectures and workshops. He also leads occasional farm tours in Korea.

We owe them both much gratitude for showing us all a better way to farm and raise food and animals in harmony with the natural world.

Mike Dupont is our local University of Hawaii - College of Tropical Agriculture and Human Resources (UH-CTAHR) Agriculture Extension agent. He has been instrumental in coaxing and encouraging us to build the piggery, even going so far as to write up a grant for the first phase of construction. He came up with the name "Hubbell Bubble" for our chicken coop design and continues to promote it throughout the islands. He is a great proponent of Korean Natural Farming.

Our Journey to Natural Farming

Mike and I met in high school, and a few months after graduation, we moved with his family to the far north of Idaho, where we lived on the same 40-acre farm for 32 years. We raised our family there, as well as chickens, livestock, huge all-organic vegetable gardens, dozens of various fruit trees, ornamentals, and an extensive herb garden. We even had a half-acre organic U-Pick strawberry field. After the children were grown, we decided to retire to Hawaii. Though we had used bio-intensive organic methods very successfully for decades, all that wonderful gardening knowledge we'd accumulated just wasn't translating well to our new home in the Puna District of Hawaii.

In the summer of 2009, we attended one of the monthly workshops at Rozett's Nursery and heard Dr Hoon Park speak about Korean Natural Farming. There were a couple other speakers as well, all practicing this method here on the wet side of the Big Island—so we knew it worked locally. Dr Park spoke of and demonstrated various techniques for creating Indigenous Micro-Organisms (IMO), which are an integral part of Natural Farming methods. This workshop was so interesting that, though the lecture was scheduled to be one-and-a-half to two hours, every attendee was still listening raptly four hours later! I took over 20 pages of notes! At the end of it all, Dr Park mentioned that he was arranging a tour to Korea that autumn, and would be happy to take anyone who was interested in seeing Korean Natural Farming in action. We looked at each other and thought, "Let's do it!"

And so, in October of that year, we joined a small group of other Big Islanders to do a Natural Farm Tour in a country that we'd never even thought about visiting before. What an opportunity! This group also included one of our County commissioners and two University of Hawaii agriculture extension agents. It was a six-night whirlwind tour of 14 farms and several farming communities across the southern countryside: ChoongNam, DangJin, DamYang, GokSeong, SoonCheon, JeonNam, GoSeong, GyungNam, and then back to Seoul. Every farm we visited utilizes the Cho Global Natural Farming (CGNF) method and is getting amazing results with vegetables, fruit orchards, rice fields, and greenhouse crops... as well as with chickens, pigs, and cows. We got the grand tour at the County Agriculture Technical Centers in both GokSeong and GoSeong Districts. We even got to see a municipal waterway in Seoul that had been transformed from a major stinky sewage canal to a lovely urban park—all by using IMO's.

It was exciting and invigorating to see how Natural Farming transformed not only fields and crops, but also the farmers themselves. To walk their orchards and barns with them while hearing their stories was truly inspiring. And we were so fortunate to have Master Cho, his wife, and his daughter with us on this tour; the reactions of these farmers, his former students, were heart-warming. We had never thought about raising pigs until we entered barns that had no foul odor and held calm sows alongside their cute little piglets sharing a large pen. This, we thought, this we could do. This is the way.

Shortly after returning from that life-changing trip, we embarked on this new phase of our so-called retirement. We were so excited to have found a natural method that we could utilize here on our own small farm in Puna. Soon we began work building the piggery, adding more chicken pens, planting an acre of tropical food crops, and making our own IMO and Natural Farming ingredients (inputs).

Our farm has been a regular feature for Community College and UHH agriculture classes, as well CGNF farm tours. This book is a compilation of the information we share with those tours.

Indigenous Micro-Organisms (IMO)

What They Are

Indigenous = local, right where you are, wherever that may be

Micro = small, tiny

Organisms = beings

IMO = the little, tiny critters that live in the soil right where you are! Microbes. Beneficial fungi, bacteria, and protozoa. These feed on the nutrients in the soil and in turn become food for earthworms, beetles, millipedes, and other small creatures that further break down soil nutrients, thus making them available for plants to feed upon.

You can do it too, anywhere & everywhere!

Many countries around the world are utilizing IMOs in the raising of crops and animals. There's no good reason why it can't be done throughout the US, too. Since they are cultivated on the spot, you can start in your own backyard, garden, homestead, or farm. After all, the "indigenous" bit means "local, right where you are, wherever that may be".

For recipes to make the inputs, information on formulas, and directions on how to use them, see Master Cho's books or the Natural Farm Hawaii group website. My chapter entitled "Further Info" has a list of these resources. Even better, attend a workshop in Natural Farming. Here, I will give just a very brief overview of the process for making IMO and the other NF inputs.

How we get them

There are several stages one goes through to get the IMO we use in the piggery and gardens. You start with a handful of rice—

white works best. You cook it not quite all the way, and cover it with leaves, touching the soil. After a few days, you check for the white fungus growing on it. That's IMO1.

To make IMO2, you mix this fungus-covered rice with brown sugar. At this point, it becomes a stable product and can be kept for a year if you don't use it for the next step right away.

IMO3 is created when you add a carbohydrate source (mill run, rice bran, or whatever is available locally) to increase the micro-organisms. You also add some of the other NF inputs and water. Your pile has increased quite a bit at this point and you need to have a cool, shady place—preferably right on the dirt—to let it sit and cultivate for about a week.

IMO4 is what we actually use. It is made by adding an equal amount of the soil where you live to the pile of IMO3. To this you also add Oriental Herbal Nutrient, Fermented Plant Juice, Brown Rice Vinegar, and seawater diluted with clear water. It'll heat up, then cool down, and then become a fairly stable product that we can use as needed in the animal pens, on the garden, or even for such things as eliminating odors in the car.

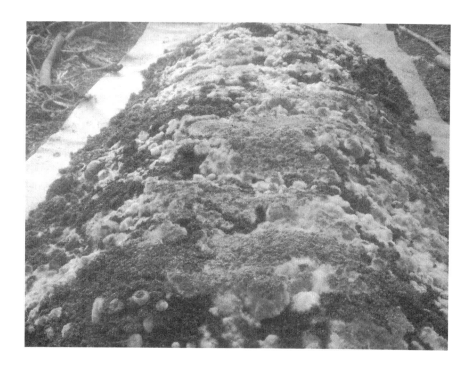

Other NF In-puts

Each of the following inputs has multiple uses in Korean Natural Farming. It's all done with whatever natural stuff you have on hand: egg shells, cooked rice, fish scraps, chopped sugar cane, weeds, bones, vinegar, ocean water... They all have their specific uses in Natural Farming.

LAB - also called "lacto" - Lactic Acid Bacteria is present everywhere and all we need to do is gather the indigenous varieties in the air all around us, wherever we are. It is our go-to remedy for any odors in the barn and any signs of illness or disease in the animals. It is abundant in the whey from yogurt and cheese-making, or it can be cultivated with rice wash water (saved from the first rinse of rice in preparation for cooking) and unpasteurized milk.

OHN - Licorice, angelica, ginger, garlic, and cinnamon are the ingredients used in the preparation of Oriental Herbal Nutrient. Used for plants, animals, and people... and by the way, it is delicious stuff!

FPJ - By taking the growing tips of whatever plant is doing super-well in your garden—whether it's a vegetable, herb, or weed—and mixing with brown sugar and letting it set a while, Fermented Plant Juice is made.

FFJ - Doing the same thing as above, but with fruit of any kind, you get Fermented Fruit Juice.

FAA - Fish Amino Acid is a liquid made from fish waste. Similar to Asian fish sauce used in food preparation, but without the added salt, it is made by mixing fish parts with brown sugar and letting it ferment for a few months.

WCA - Water-soluble Calcium is made from roasted eggshells soaked in brown rice vinegar.

WCP - Water-soluble Calcium-Phosphate comes from clean bones that have been burned in a low fire, then soaked in brown rice vinegar.

BRV - Brown Rice Vinegar raises the calcium absorption ratio.

Seawater, dipped from the ocean, is used diluted with fresh water to add minerals, for soil treatment before seeding, and to enhance ripening of fruit.

Biochar, a fine-grained, highly porous charcoal, provides a storehouse for all the nutrients and microbes so that it stays readily available for your plants when they need them.

The Piggery

We built the barn with breeding pigs in mind, as opposed to raising pigs up to market size. There are six 12 foot by 12 foot pens; one of them is being used for tool storage. Each pen is large enough for a sow and her piglets up to weaning age. The floor level inside the barn is three feet off the ground because we are on broken pahoehoe lava rock—we can't dig down very easily, so we went up instead. We used treated wood and heavy corrugated metal siding because Mike was more comfortable using those materials, but you can easily use whatever building materials you like: cement, concrete blocks, rock wall, or whatever.

Master Cho's barn design has a sliding roof to allow the sun to shine directly on the bedding as it moves through the sky. The ultraviolet light can help rid the bedding of harmful bacteria. But there were some problems with this design for us here on the rainy side of the island. What we did instead was to put in a strip of clear plastic roofing panels directly above each pen. The rest of the roof is made of translucent white roofing panels, allowing plenty of brightness. We wouldn't use the clear panels again, because there's no UV coming through that plastic anyway, and at the same time there's more heat build-up with the sunlight coming through. Pigs like it cool. A possible solution to the UV conundrum would be to use the polycarbonate panels that are specially formulated to allow UV to pass through; however, they're costly, hard to find, and we haven't tried them yet.

Another thing that makes this particular piggery special is the liner. Instead of the usual cement, each pen was lined with a woven geotextile plastic groundcover-like fabric. This is to keep the rocks and cinder from puncturing the actual liner, which is a thick woven polyethylene waterproof material. Using a waterproof liner like this is not part of the CGNF method. Ideally, there would be direct contact with the soil. However, in the US, there is great concern over groundwater pollution, so hoops must be jumped through. Our piggery was the pilot project for using something other than concrete to line a deep litter system. We had to get special permission from the US Department of Agriculture, National Soil & Water Conservation. Our "ag guy", Mike Dupont, was an invaluable help in getting the necessary permissions for us to proceed.

Airflow is Important

Fresh air flows in from low on the sides, moves across the floor, and goes up and out the center clerestory in the roof. This keeps the inside of the barn cool and fresh, removing excess moisture and heat as it flows. We take advantage of the tradewinds by partially covering the sides with shade cloth, rather than enclosing them all the way with something more solid. It does slightly reduce the airflow, but has the advantages of stopping most of the windblown rain and of providing shade. Pink-skinned pigs get sunburned; the shade cloth helps prevent that.

Built-in Scale

One end of the walkway is a built-in platform scale. Mike put this together with a kit he bought online. The kit came with four load cells with feet attached, a junction box, and a readout panel. He mounted it all to a 2x6 frame under one of the sheets of plywood we used for the walkway. Thus, this one section was left free-floating on the feet of the scales. It's easy to run a pig down the walkway to monitor weight-gain or to weigh before selling.

Water Systems

We have tried many watering devices in search of one that allows the pigs easy access to plentiful water to drink, and at the same time will not overflow or run freely onto the bedding. Wet bedding causes anaerobic conditions to develop, and it gets pretty stinky when that happens. Pigs do love to wallow in a puddle, though, and they'll figure out any way they can to create a mudhole. They're pretty smart that way!

Currently, we use nipple waterers. At first we had them fixed to the wall, but it was too easy for the pigs to make a mess. We rigged up a piece of 4" PVC pipe around the nipple, so that the pig would have to put its snout in there to drink and the excess water would run down the pipe and outside the pen, away from the bedding. They figured out a way around that, too, somehow.

Then we tried a special kind of nipple waterer that has to go further into the pig's mouth before they can bite it to start the water flow. This didn't work at all; the bedding particles got stuck between the ball they had to bite on and the nipple, thereby keeping the water flowing freely even without the pigs' help.

We quickly took those out and replaced them with a hanging waterer. The theory behind this kind is that, since it takes more concentration for the pigs to hold it in their mouth (because it can swing around), they wouldn't play with it as long. It was a partial success. These smart piggies figured out how to bite on and let the water run out of their mouth and down their chest, so we still got the wet bedding problem, but not as badly. We had to rake out the wet spot now and then, to let it dry out. On the whole, this system was an improvement, but still, we looked for a better way.

The current watering system is fixed to a post and has a stainless steel bowl with a nipple valve. The pigs get water by pressing against this valve with their nose. The bowl then catches the water and the pigs suck it up in a more natural manner, as their wild cousins would do out of a puddle. The theory here is that this waterer will not overflow because pigs can't hold their breath long enough for the water to run over the rim. So far, so good.

Filling the Pens

On a fine early February morning in 2011, several folks from our local Natural Farming group came out to help with filling the first pen. It was a very hands-on way to learn how to create the various layers needed for the microbes to thrive.

First, we set down six inches of red Hamakua cinder-soil, and topped that with one cubic foot of biochar spread thinly over the soil. On this base we placed an assortment of logs, gleaned off our property. Most of them were albezia and secropia, but there were a few ohia and others in there as well. The logs ranged from six inches to one foot in diameter.

With our chipper/shredder we had prepared wood chips from the smaller branches and coconut husks to use for filling in around the logs. These went in next, with palm fronds laid over the top.

Atop this mass of plant material, we added nine tractor-scoops of sawdust to each single scoop of cinder soil. These ingredients were somewhat mixed as they got raked into the corners of the pen. The sawdust came from a local mill and is made of tropical hardwoods, but of course you would use whatever local resource you have. Each layer got sprinkled with IMO4, sea salt, and more biochar, according to Master Cho's formula. We did several layers like this to fill the pen, raking out between scoops to keep it nicely leveled.

A week later, we added about one pound of dolomite and more IMO4. Each week for the next three months, we spread more IMO4 and sprayed the floor with one gallon water, to which had been added one teaspoon FPJ and one teaspoon LAB.

By the time we got to the third pen, we had learned more about the microbes and were filling them a little differently. First, we went about halfway up with the logs, then we added the biochar and lots of coconut husks before adding the other layers. We used some partially decomposed sawdust, mixed with ten percent cinder-soil. That was topped with fresh wood chips from a pile of branches and smaller trees we had here. Mike chipped up greenwaste and mixed that with the cindersoil, too. The IMO4 and sea salt were sprinkled into the very top layer, which the pigs mixed in as they rooted around. Nice of them to help, don't you think?

One problem we noticed is that the decomposing sawdust created quite a bit of heat. This would be ideal in a cooler climate (like Korea), but we are in the tropics and at a fairly low elevation (400'). We switched to using woodchips instead. This slows the decomposition, thereby creating less heat for the pigs.

At first, we tried a misting system that got turned on during hot days. The fine mist spray really helped the sows keep their cool, but wreaked havoc on the bedding, increasing decomposition and causing anaerobic bacteria to flourish, thus creating more smell and flies. We took the mist system out and now on hot days we'll deliver a fine mist of LAB on the piggies using a handheld garden sprayer. They sure do enjoy it and it helps them—and the whole IMO system—maintain health.

How We Utilize IMO in the Piggery

Pen maintenance is easy. The floor gets raked every morning while the pigs are feeding, and once in a while the extra coconut husks are picked up. For a while, more IMO4 was sprinkled weekly over the fresh manure to help it break down more quickly. This is no longer needed because there is enough microbial and fungal life in the pen to do the job. Whenever we add new woodchips to the pen to bring the ground level back up—and this is far more often than we thought it would be!—more IMO4 and LAB are added.

For the rare times when there are excess flies, more IMO4 is sprinkled on top. And any time there is a health issue, LAB is sprayed. It can go directly on pigs, piglets, bedding, food... just cover as much area as possible with a fine mist spray.

No waste treatment is necessary because there is no waste. The microbes are taking care of that constantly, right in place.

Mostly, we just get to hang out with the girls and give them pets and attention, which they absolutely love! And that's pretty much it! No smell, very few flies. Contented, happy, healthy pigs. That's what it's all about.

Approved!

In August 2012, as part of the Swine Seminar held in Hilo, Hog Heaven was one of three local piggeries chosen for the field trip portion of the seminar. Among the participants were officials from Hawaii State's Puna Soil & Water Conservation District, and, at the Federal level, the USDA and the NRCS.

Adam Reed is the guy who's in charge of rewriting and updating the laws regarding the housing aspects of swine production on a national level. He was very interested in and very pleased with what he saw here at Hubbell's Hog Heaven, and he has recommended that the Korean Natural Farming method of raising pigs—this system of incorporating deep bedding along with beneficial microbes, and using a thick woven plastic liner (as opposed to concrete)—be written into the new federal guidelines as a "best management practice".

As of January 2013, it is now legal for others across the entire United States to raise commercial pigs this way. This is huge!! Needless to say, we are quite pleased. Mission accomplished!

The Pigs

First Natural Farmed Litter in Hawaii & the United States!

We didn't know it at the time, but we were told by our University of Hawaii Agriculture Extension agent that not only did we have our own first litter of piglets—born on the 4th of July, 2011—but they were also the first litter of pigs born into the Korean Natural Farming method in Hawaii and, in fact, in the entire USA! There were other piggeries using the Natural Farm method, based on Master Cho's teachings, but they weren't doing the breeding aspect of pig-raising.

We no longer have our original sows, but our current breed sows, Spot and Big Mama, are from that first litter. Their piglets constitute the second generation of NF born and bred pigs. Both are excellent mothers with their natural instincts intact—meaning that they are responsive to their babies, so there are fewer worries about accidental squishing. They also have good conformity for nursing, with ample milk supplies. We couldn't be more pleased about that!

Artificial Insemination, AI

We've been using semen from the boars at UH-Hilo's Panaewa research farm. This way, we don't have to keep a boar and we have the option of choosing which breed characteristics we're aiming for. Most breeds in the US these days have been bred to do better in confinement operations and factory 'farms', and to have a leaner meat. This is the exact opposite of what we want!

So we breed for good mothering instincts as well as good physical conformation. Healthy fat is really very good for us. If we feed our pigs a healthy diet (what they are designed to eat in nature) we do not need to be afraid of eating their meat or fat.

Don't do the AI too early (or too late). The sows come into heat every three weeks until they are bred. Since the physical characteristics of heat can be subtle, you need to know your pigs well enough to notice changes in their behavior as well. You have a 12-hour window to get the best results (i.e., the most piglets). You want to aim for two inseminations during that peak time. You can learn a lot more about it on YouTube—that's how we taught ourselves.

We keep getting asked how long a pig's gestation period is. The answer is a fun one to say: three months, three weeks, and three days.

Farrowing

Sadly, in the US, most pigs are raised in industrialized confinement operations, where everything goes against their natural instincts. They are confined in narrow stalls, unable to move freely, and their mothering instincts are being bred out of them. We have been working to breed these good mothering instincts back in to our pigs. In Korean Natural Farming, we don't use farrowing crates or stalls. The mother moves freely in her large pen, making her nest when she is ready, shifting positions as she wishes. Since her piglets stay with her, mama sow must be responsive to their squeals so that she'll get up right away if she accidentally lies on one. The piglets thrive, even without heat lamps or a creep area.

A month or so before farrowing is due, we add enough wood chips to top off the sows' pens. We want to make sure the pen is well-inoculated before birthing begins, so we add a sprinkling of IMO4 and spray the surface with LAB to ensure a proliferation of beneficial bacteria before the piglets are born. We repeat the IMO4 and LAB applications just before birthing.

Be forewarned: DO NOT add fresh wood chips right before farrowing! Warm, wet wood chips that haven't yet been inoculated with IMOs harbor the bacteria that causes mastitis. We learned this the hard way. Both our girls, one after the other, got sick with high fever, inflamed udders, and loss of appetite. They just lay in misery, ignoring their piglets because they were so delirious with fever. Mike had to go out to the barn every hour, night and day, to prod them until they rolled over to nurse their piglets. Sadly, Spot lost one of her piglets during this time. Mastitis is serious stuff. We had to give the sows penicillin injections, spray them and their pens with LAB, and spread IMO4 all over the bedding like crazy. In a few days they were back on their feet, eating, and nursing well again—thank goodness! So, don't use fresh green woodchips, and do use penicillin if/when it is necessary.

Restrict the sow's feed the day farrowing is due. She will have a much easier time of it without a belly full of food. Her appetite should come back the day after delivery, if not sooner. At that time she starts getting extra feed to accommodate her extra nutritional and caloric needs during lactation. We divide her feed, so she'll get some in the morning and the larger half in the late afternoons.

The mama sow and her piglets get sprayed with LAB a couple times after farrowing to help prevent disease. We often sprinkle a little extra IMO during delivery, in between babies, to help keep the flies down. The entire pen is sprinkled with IMO4 and sprayed with LAB, both before and after the birth. We don't give inoculations; we let the IMOs keep the animals healthy.

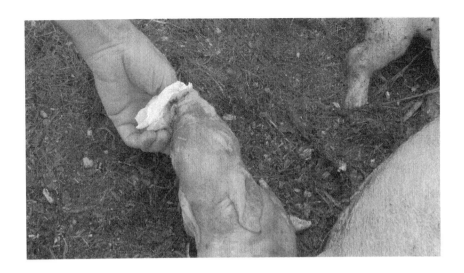

Piglets get their nose and mouth wiped clean right away so they can begin breathing. The rest of the sac is allowed to break away and fall apart as the piglet moves about; the IMOs help with that process, too. The umbilical cord breaks naturally as baby is delivered, leaving a long "tail" from the piglet's belly. This, too, will dry up on its own. On the rare occasions when there is a hemorrhage, the cord gets tied off with a piece of string at an inch or so from the belly. This has happened only once, so far, but it goes to illustrate why it is so important to be present for farrowing.

Placentas are buried in the pen with a sprinkling of IMO4. She will likely dig up and eat at least some of it, and that's okay. It is full of iron and protein that will help her gain back her strength after delivery.

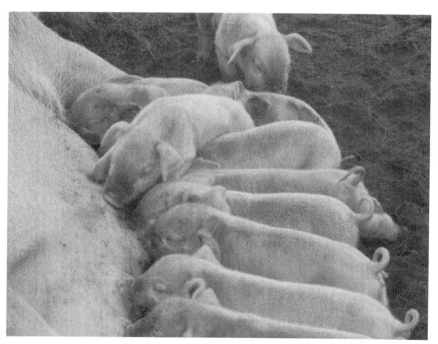

Caring for Piglets

Piglets get their eye teeth nipped off within the first day. There is a special tool for this that makes it easier, and safer for the babies. We usually leave the smaller piglets' eye teeth intact to help them have a better chance at nursing time. Piglets can be very aggressive when it comes to finding their place at the nipple line, and their cute little noses will soon be covered with cuts and scratches from their littermates. The IMO and LAB ever-present in the pens help to keep them from becoming infected.

When the piglets are about two weeks old, we add a creep area by fencing off a corner of the pen with a gate panel that has openings wide enough for the piglets to pass through, but not big enough for the sow's head to reach in. Now the babies have a chance to eat their feed before mama gets to it all. The piglets start out with however much feed they can finish off in about 15 minutes, twice a day, when mama gets fed.

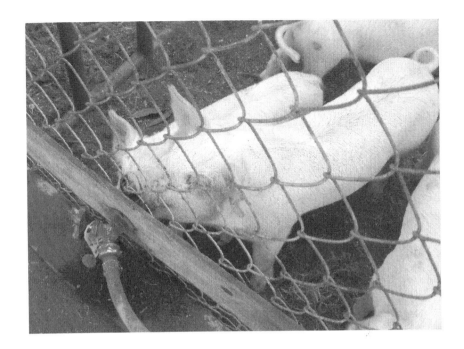

We also add a nipple waterer in the creep area, mounted down low, so they can start learning how to use it. They are curious and begin to play with it, and it seems that as soon as one learns how it works, all the rest figure it out by imitating.

Their feed will increase gradually as they—and their appetites!—get bigger. The piglets get weaned at six weeks, when mama gets moved to another pen. They'll be eating enough regular feed by then to make the transition easily. The wean-offs are usually sold within a week. They are well over 30 pounds by then.

Feeding Pigs

The pig's natural diet is omnivorous and opportunistic. It is filled with such high-protein delicacies as grubs and earthworms. Wild pigs will feast on fallen fruits, roots, and even carrion as they come across such things. We are attempting to mimic the amounts of protein, vitamins, and minerals present in this diet. We'd like to include grubs and earthworms, but have yet to come up with a non-labor-intensive method of doing so.

Once a day, each sow gets four and a half pounds of pelleted pig feed. (**NOTE**: This is why we are working so hard on raising our own crops, to replace this store-bought feed and still maintain the proper protein, amino acids, and nutrient levels. We're getting there, but we're not there yet. Mostly, we're waiting for the plants to grow bigger, and of course, planting more crops.)

To this feed, we add a handful of IMO4 to keep them healthy, and it has the added benefit of making their poops break down super fast. Also in the mix is at least one or two pounds of fresh greens—sweet potato tops, sunn hemp, and honohono grass are current favorites. On the side, they get a half a coconut each, as well as sugar cane stalks chopped into foot-long pieces. (Interestingly, since we started feeding sugarcane we haven't needed to refill the pens nearly as often; the pigs chew the cane and spit out the bagasse, which makes excellent bedding.) They get the leaves of sugar cane, too—we just give them the whole top, as well as the chopped cane part.

Sometimes, as a treat, there is papaya, avocado, kabocha, guava, or whatever might be in abundance. We don't feed these fruits and vegetables exclusively though, as many hereabouts do, because pigs need protein and fats to really thrive, and that's what we're aiming for—their long term health. Occasionally, we will toss them an egg or two, which gets chomped right down, shell and all.

A word of **caution** on gathering wild greens: Know what you're gathering! For example, wadelia grows abundantly around here, and though it looks so nice and lush, with its glossy dark green leaves and sunny yellow flowers, **DO NOT** feed it to pigs, especially not to pregnant sows. It is an abortificant, so beware. (It doesn't seem to bother the chickens though.) We are extremely careful about picking out any stray runners of this plant when gathering the daily greens.

During the last three weeks of pregnancy, the sow's feed gradually increases until she's getting about seven and a half to eight pounds a day. Those piglets are growing fast by then, and she's also building up the mammary tissue.

When a sow starts nursing, her diet will change to accommodate her increased needs and ensure a good milk supply. The feed increases to four and a half to six pounds commercial feed, plus another one pound per piglet she's nursing. So, for a litter of ten, mama will get 14-1/2 to 16 pounds of feed each day. At this time, we divide her total intake of feed to two times a day so that she can finish it all without distress. The larger feeding happens later in the day, usually a couple hours before sunset. More greens will be added, too.

The Chickens

I have always raised chickens. I could not imagine not having at least a small backyard flock. So, once we were settled in, I asked Mike to build me a chicken yard. We didn't have to worry about coyotes, weasels, owls, or large raptors here in Hawaii, but we do have a different assortment of predators...

There are mongoose and rats coming in from the jungle. We also have a family of 'Io, the small endemic hawk, nearby, so we needed to protect our birds from aerial attacks, too. And stray dogs were a problem that has since been taken care of by the perimeter fence.

Since we are on broken pahoehoe lava, we can't dig into the ground. However, the climate is mild enough to make raising poultry particularly easy. Chickens don't really mind rain at all, but the pen itself will be far less stinky if it is kept dry. They enjoy a dust bath to help keep mites under control; that is another benefit of a dry yard for the birds. And by keeping it dry, the rich soil in the coop is available for use as fertilizer without it being washed away with each downpour. At the same time, we don't want to harbor rats, cockroaches, or other tropical pests... and we do want the birds out in the fresh air and sunshine.

Mike took all these considerations and came up with a nice little covered chicken yard that includes a skirting to foil the mongoose from digging underneath. We later incorporated a nest box that can be accessed from the outside of the pen, to make it much easier to collect eggs.

Hubbell Bubble Coop Design

When our ag guy, Mike Dupont, first dropped by our place in 2009 to take a look at our little backyard farm, he was so taken with our coop design that he immediately dubbed it "The Hubbell Bubble". He asked if Mike was going to patent the plan, and Mike said no, it was an idea to be shared freely. At Mr Dupont's instigation, UH-CTAHR adopted it as their model to promote backyard chicken-raising. We were a little dazed at all the attention, but certainly ready and willing to help. And it's always nice to be recognized for a good idea.

In February 2010, the first public demo coop was constructed during Ka Uluana: Securing Our Future Food Resilience Project at the Kohala Intergenerational Center in Kapa'au. Since then, we have built many Bubbles for other events and groups such as The Boys and Girls Club of Hilo, Panaewa Farmers, and the 2010 Cho Global Conference in Hilo, as well as for individuals. Others have spread the word and built their own Bubbles, taking the plans with them to the other islands and even other countries!

As we've built more of our own chicken areas, we have adjusted the design of the coop a bit, making changes as needed and utilizing whatever materials we have on hand, as any good homesteader would do.

The second chicken coop (above, on the right) is one such variation on the Hubbell Bubble theme. This one still has the anti-mongoose skirting and the roof over the entire yard for both hawk and rain protection. But, since we utilized building materials we already had lying about the place, it's got 2x4's and the roof is made of scrap pieces of tin, with a small vent space at the peak. Another difference is that we ran the chicken wire horizontally around the entire pen, rather than covering each individual panel vertically as in the original Bubble plan. This made stapling it on much easier. The wiring runs in two tiers, with the bottom of the lower tier becoming the skirting.

Furnishing the Coop

Besides the usual store-bought products, Mike has come up with some unique designs using what we have lying about. PVC pipe and elbows and extra rain gutters have become feeders; cut-off plastic jugs and drip irrigation line were some of our original chicken waterers; and the ubiquitous waiwi/strawberry guava makes excellent roosts.

Nest boxes are made the same way: with whatever bits and pieces we have. There are several different designs currently in use, and all of them back up to an outside wall of the chicken yard for easy collecting of eggs. They have a piece of shade cloth to create a dark space for the chickens to feel secluded and safe while eggs are being laid. Group nest boxes are ideal for these social birds. For nesting material, we use whatever dry plant material is at hand: bamboo leaves, ferns, wood chips or sawdust, leaves, and the like.

The water buckets are 5-gallon plastic buckets with three chicken nipple waterers drilled into the bottom. The chickens learn to use these fairly quickly; as soon as one figures it out, the rest follow suit. This is the least wasteful way we've found for watering chickens, which is always a consideration, but especially if you have to haul water. To refill, simply lift the lid and insert a garden hose.

Feeding Chickens

Every day the birds get a can of scratch. I fill their feeders with lay pellets, and they also get kitchen scraps and trimmings. Since they are in a yard, I bring the greens to them. Each coop gets a bucketful of weeds and greens: sweet potato tops, kabocha leaves, banana leaves, moringa, fallen guava... whatever is abundant and available. They get a split open coconut, too.

The Flock

The older flock of two- and three-year-olds has 14 hens, and the younger flock of 60 started laying in February 2013. I like to have a mixed flock of many breeds—just a personal preference.

The Pearl Leghorns are small white birds with the highest feed to egg conversion ratio; they lay large white-shelled eggs.

Rhode Island Reds are very popular around here and lay large brown eggs.

Auracanas or Americanas are the "Easter egg" chickens with shells of blues and greens.

Barred Rocks are larger striped birds that lay white eggs.

Buff Orpingtons are larger golden birds with a calm temperament; they make perfect broody hens and they lay large brown eggs.

A scattering of other breeds are mixed in for variety and beauty. With this assortment I get a nice variety of colored eggs to mix in each dozen I sell—the customers like that!

Eggs

I gather eggs twice a day: in the mornings at feeding time, and in the late afternoon; this gives the hens plenty of time to lay undisturbed. I wash the eggs with water only, and only as needed, to help preserve the waxy outer coating on the shells; the coating helps the eggs stay fresh much longer. Store eggs with the narrow pointy end down; they'll keep for a longer time that way, as the air sack inside won't break down as quickly.

Egg production slows quite a bit with the shorter days of winter, even here in Hawaii. Chickens need 12 hours of daylight to trigger laying. They will come into full production again in the springtime.

Occasionally, chickens go through a molting cycle where they lose more feathers than usual and stop laying eggs. Their feathers will grow back and they'll come into production again in a month or two.

In Hawaii, we have found hens to be good egg-layers for only about two to three years. At peak production, and depending on the breed, you can expect each hen to lay four to six eggs a week. They may continue to lay after that, but it tapers off quickly.

Raising Chicks

You can order chicks from Asagi Hatchery on O'ahu, or get them from your local feed store or other farmers nearby. You can let a hen go broody if you have a rooster in the flock for fertile eggs. Or you can procure fertile eggs, either from your own hens or by buying them, and then let an incubator do the brooding for you. The advantage of the incubator method is that it won't change its mind halfway through incubation, which takes 28 days.

Regardless of how they were hatched, after their first 24 hours, chicks are transferred to our version of Master Cho's brood pen. Mike built this using bits and pieces we had lying about on the farm: some old Trex decking, a piece of plywood, 2x2 lumber, and hardware cloth (screen). The brood pen has two parts to it: one section is covered with a plywood top, and the other section has a screen top. A third section can be added for more room as the chicks grow. The tops of each section lift off for easy access to the birds (for feeding, changing water, and so on).

Underneath the plywood-topped section, a hole is dug and fresh compost is buried. The floor is gently sloped up towards the back. This allows the chicks to choose their comfort level of warmth, and no heat light is needed at all. The front of this section has a cloth hanging down to imitate the mother's wing. As the baby chicks pass under the cloth, it caresses their back and this action calms them.

Feed and water are placed at the far end of the open area so that the young birds must move and strengthen their muscles. We feed our chicks according to Master Cho's method, which is very different from what I'd been used to, but it works well and the chickens are healthy and strong. For the first three days, they are fed raw brown rice kernels, all they can eat. After that, they get chick starter and chopped grasses and IMO4. They also get hard-cooked egg yolk at this time, each day for two weeks. Of course, clean drinking water is always provided.

Once they pass the peeping stage, the chicks can be moved out to a Hubbell Bubble of their own. It will take five to six months, depending on the breed, before a pullet becomes a laying hen.

Old Birds

Any excess roosters go into the cookpot. Their pretty feathers are saved for various crafts; sometimes I sell them or give them to friends for their artwork, and some are simply displayed for their beauty.

After several years, when the hens are no longer productive, they get put on free-range "bug patrol" until they become stewing chickens.

IMO on the Land

What We're Working With Here

The ground at our farm is broken pahoehoe lava rock, with only a half-inch of topsoil, at most... but the jungle grows well, so we know it can sustain vegetation. Volcanic soils are rich in minerals, but these minerals are not easily accessible. Tree roots find the cracks in the lava, and leaves, ferns, grasses, and other flora decompose into soil. We work with Nature's system and give it a boost with IMO.

Instead of bringing in heavy equipment to rip the rock and bulldoze the jungle, we first cut out any "weed" trees. These are run through the chipper/shredder for use as chips in the pig pens. We like to keep the native ohia in place; we'll work around them. The next step is to mow and flatten the brush. We repeat this mowing as needed, and this way we get a head start on soil building. Eventually, grasses take over, which can be used for feed.

When we're ready to plant an area, we cover the ground, weeds and all, with a generous layer of plant material mulch, known hereabouts as "green waste". We make it at least six inches and up to a foot deep, depending on the crop to be planted. We'll sprinkle on some IMO4, too, to inoculate the area. The plant rows themselves get a handful of fertilizer, on the surface, which is simply scooped-up bedding from either the pigpens or the chicken coop floor.

It's important to add IMOs to the surface, not bury them in the soil, since the microbes thrive in an aerobic situation and will not do as well if they are buried. In fact, it is important not to disturb the soil at all. We want to protect the delicate balance of life in the soil ecosystem. All inputs are added to the top surface only, or on the plants themselves.

By increasing the micro-organisms and using them to speed up the decomposition of organic substances, we are thereby creating enzymes and making nutrients more available to the plants. This, in turn, balances the ecosystem and increases the productivity of the garden. Everybody wins! It's a very good compliment to the organic farming we've long done—an enhancement really, to make everything and everybody grow that much better.

Feed Crops We're Growing

We're not trying to grow mainland-type feed crops here. Grains, while they can be grown on a small scale in Hawaii, are not easy to produce here. Corn grows well but it is not part of a pig's natural diet.

What we are doing is finding what works in the tropics. We can learn a lot from other tropical countries, and we can combine plant sources to create a nutritional balance for our animals. Most of what we've chosen to grow as feed crops on our farm are perennial plants, many are trees, and all are already available on the Big Island.

We have two kinds of **sugarcane (ko)** : white and purple. We've found the white to have larger canes and more juice, but the purple is so pretty and doesn't fall over as easily. They have different tastes, too. We like them both. Studies from Cuba show that sugarcane can provide up to 80% of a pig's diet. It can be their primary source of carbohydrate, and when the entire stalk is fed to them, they are getting lots of vitamins and minerals as well.

Mulberry is grown mostly for its leaves, though the berries are quite tasty, too. It has a high protein content and helps regulate glycemic levels. The leaves are particularly digestible because of their low amounts of tannin, making their protein more readily available. (Another way to break down the tannins common in most leaf crops is to ferment them with IMOs.)

Moringa (**malunguy** in Filipino) is another high-protein leaf. It also has a high content of vitamins and minerals, making it an excellent balancing element in the total diet. But its leaves are very small, and thus it is hard to harvest enough to use as a primary feed. It does, however, make an excellent FPJ, and is sprayed as a foliar feed. All parts of the plant can be eaten. We're keeping most of these short for repeated harvests of the leaves and twigs.

Cassava (yuca or manioc as it's called in other parts of the world) is the source of tapioca. That comes from the starchy root, but it is grown for its leaves as well, which are the third component of our leafy green protein trio. It is not susceptible to the usual plant pests found in the tropics.

We grow the sweet variety of cassava. If you have the other kind, allow the fresh-cut leaves to wilt in the sun for a day before feeding to reduce the cyanide-forming compound natural to this plant.

Sunn hemp is the first thing seeded whenever a new planting area is prepared. It grows quickly, smothering out the weeds, and it is a nitrogen-fixer so it helps fertilize the soil. Once it reaches two feet high, we begin to cut it back a bit for animal feed.

When the plant is spent (it's not a perennial) we mow it down for mulch, but leave the roots in place so as not to disturb the soil. This allows the nitrogen nodules on the roots to stay available as fertilizer.

The word hemp, by the way, indicates that it was used for rope-making.

Two varieties of **sweet potatoes ('uala)**, purple and white, are grown for both tops and tubers. The white variety grows tops really fast, giving us lots of greens. They help smother out the weeds a bit, too. There's quite a bit of protein in the leaf, as well as lots of vitamins and minerals.

We can also feed the tubers to the pigs, but we get first pick! The chickens don't care for the tubers unless they are cooked.

Yes, we have lots of **bananas (mai'a)**! Bananas are a good source of minerals. All parts of the plant can be used: leaves, flowers, and fruit can be fed directly to both pigs and chickens. (And of course, we love them, too!)

Chop the stalk, mix it with IMO4 and let it set 12-24 hours; then feed it to the pigs.

Green, unripe bananas should never be fed to pigs.

Because bananas are such heavy feeders, they need a lot more fertilizer than our other crops; fortunately, there is plenty from the pigpen and chicken coop.

We are growing two varieties of **breadfruit: Hawaiian 'ulu** & **Samoan ma'afala**. The ma'afala is a smaller tree, producing smaller fruits more quickly. Not much of a protein plant, breadfruit nevertheless provides a wide assortment of vitamins and minerals, as well as complex carbohydrates.

This long-lived tree has long been an important staple of Pacific culture, providing food for both animals and people. We can hardly wait for our first fruits to appear!

And then there is the ever-present tropical **coconut (niu)**—so good for us and our animals. It will be the prime source of necessary healthy fats in our animal feed. Coconuts are easily fed to pigs and chickens by simply splitting them in half with a machete; no need to husk first. They can be used at any stage, from green water-filled, to spongy or hard fruit, to sprouted. The chickens especially love the ones with bugs or maggots in them.

Fresh coconut water is fed to piglets and to sick animals; just mix it with their feed and they'll gobble it right down.

All these (except the sunn hemp) feed us as well as the animals.

One thing to note, and I guess this is as good a place as any to mention it, is that we have a woven wire perimeter fence encircling the entire farm. This serves to keep out stray dogs that would otherwise harm our animals, as well as the wild pigs that would be attracted to the sweet potato, cassava, guava, and the like.

Our Aim

- To not have to rely on shipped-in, store-bought animal feed for the pigs and chickens, while still providing balanced feeds that meet their ideal nutritional requirements.

- To produce more of our own healthy food.

- To encourage others to do the same.

.

Further Info

We have hosted farm tours for many groups who want to learn more about Korean Natural Farming, and to see it in action here in Hawaii. Several classes from UH-Hilo have come through, as well as smaller groups and individuals from all over the world. Some of the officials we visited in South Korea returned the favor and visited us in October 2011. If you would like to arrange a farm tour, give us a call at 808-965-8235. Or you can email Mike at mike@myhawaiianrental.com

Feel free to follow my piggery blog with sporadic updates on the progress of Hubbell's Hog Heaven:
HubbellsHogHeaven.blogspot.com

For detailed information on Korean Natural Farming, including the formulas and recipes for creating your own IMO and inputs, see Master Cho's books:

Natural Farming, 2010

Cho Han Kyu's Natural Farming, 2003

...and his daughter, Cho Ju-Young, who now runs the Janong Natural Farming Institute, has written: *Natural Farming: Agriculture materials*, 2010

Their website: **janonglove.com/janongusa/index.html**

Gil Carandang, a leader in Natural Farming in the Philippines, gives a more tropical approach in his book:

Grow Your Own Beneficial Indigenous Microorganismas and Bionutrients in Natural Farming, by Gil A Carandang, 2011

UH-CTAHR has printed up a brochure with plans and a materials list for the original Hubbell Bubble Chicken Coop, available at the University Extension offices in Hilo.

Our local Natural Farm group holds monthly meeting in Hilo, on the second Tuesday each month at 6:00 pm. Anyone who is interested is welcome to attend. Check the website for the location, topic, and potluck info, as well as a plethora of NF related information: **naturalfarminghawaii.net**

We also run a vacation rental house, and many of our guests choose to stay with us specifically because of their interest in Natural Farming, and for the opportunity to see it first-hand. If you are interested in booking a stay with us, see our website for Hale Pomaika'i, the House of Good Fortune. We would be happy to accommodate you!

MyHawaiianRental.com

Made in the USA
Columbia, SC
30 December 2017